Hua Hu Ching

The Unknown Teachings of
LAO TZU

T0073034

Hua Hu Ching

The Unknown Teachings of
LAO TZU

BRIAN WALKER

HarperOne
An Imprint of HarperCollinsPublishers

HarperOne

HarperCollins Web site: http://www.harpercollins.com

HarperCollins®, 📖®, and HarperOne™ are trademarks of
HarperCollins Publishers.

FIRST HARPERCOLLINS PAPERBACK EDITION PUBLISHED IN 1995

Library of Congress Cataloging-in-Publication Data
is available upon request.
ISBN 978-0-06-069245-2

HB 01.23.2024

Dedication

This book is dedicated to a mob of unruly angels. It is as much theirs as it is mine:

To my parents, Bud and Joan, who gave me life, love, and an understanding of the spiritual importance of silliness;

To the memory of my maternal grandmother, Cynthia Pace Radcliffe, who walks beside me wherever I go, fire eating fire;

To the memory of Edward Abbey, bone of my bone and blood of my heart: Hoka Hey, Grandfather!

To Jim Harrison, the Conquering Lion of Northern Michigan;

To Stephen Mitchell, bridge across time for so many sacred flames;

And, finally, with a large and unyielding love, to my gentle, graceful daughter, Sofia Sofia Muhammad Ali: dance on, little laughing crow.

Acknowledgments

I have come to think of Lao Tzu less as a man who once lived and more as a song that plays, eternal and abiding. I am deeply indebted to Martin Gray, George Robinson, and Master Ni Hua-Ching, for bringing me into the presence of the song once again.

Jamie Potenberg and Stacy Feldmann designed this book, provoking appreciative murmurs all the way from my house to the Realm of the Immortals. Russell Chatham made it possible for them to do so, for which I thank him.

My heartfelt appreciation goes also to my father and mother, without whose generous support and gentle teachings none of my books would be.

Finally, my deepest gratitude goes to my beloved teacher and provocative friend, Valerie Haumont, who has led me to and traveled with me through a generous assortment of the Ten Thousand Spiritual Supernovas, Endless Voids, and Black Holes. In those illuminating and terrifying places I gained the understanding necessary to write this book. May I yet have the grace to come to live it.

> The flute of interior time plays,
> whether we hear it or not.
> What we mean by love is its sound coming in.
>
> ROBERT BLY, *BOOK OF KABIR*

On waking after the accident
I was presented with the "whole picture"
as they say, magnificently detailed,
a child's diorama of what life appears to be:
staring at the picture I became drowsy
with relief when I noticed a yellow
dot of light in the lower right-hand corner.
I unhooked the machines and tubes and crawled
to the picture, with an eyeball to the dot
of light which turned out to be a miniature
tunnel at the end of which I could see
mountains and stars whirling and tumbling,
sheets of emotions, vertical rivers, upside
down lakes, herds of unknown mammals, birds
shedding feathers and regrowing them instantly,
snakes with feathered heads eating their own
shed skins, fish swimming straight up,
the bottom of Isaiah's robe, live whales
on dry ground, lions drinking from a golden
bowl of milk, the rush of night,
and somewhere in this the murmur of gods—
a tree-rubbing-tree music, a sweet howl
of water and rock-grating-rock, fire
hissing from fissures, the moon settled
comfortably on the ground, beginning to roll.

JIM HARRISON, FROM *THE THEORY AND
PRACTICE OF RIVERS*

The *Tao te Ching* of Lao Tzu is among the most widely translated and cherished books in the world. Singular in its lucidity, revered across cultural boundaries for its timeless wisdom, it is believed among Westerners to be Lao Tzu's only book. Few are aware that a collection of his oral teachings on the subject of attaining enlightenment and mastery were also recorded in a book called the *Hua Hu Ching* (pronounced "wha hoo jing").

The teachings of the *Hua Hu Ching* are of enormous power and consequence, a literal road map to the divine realm for ordinary human beings. Perhaps predictably, the book was banned during a period of political discord in China, and all copies were ordered to be burned. Were it not for the Taoist tradition of oral transmission of sacred scriptures from master to student, they would have been lost forever. I am permanently indebted to Taoist Master Ni Hua-Ching for sharing his version of these teachings with the Western world after his emigration from China in 1976. My work here is largely based upon his teaching.

I bow also to Stephen Mitchell, whose recent translation of the *Tao te Ching* moved, shaped, and informed me. I encourage readers of this volume to also study Stephen's book; his elucidation of the Tao and how it manifests in the world is exquisite.

It would be a profound pleasure to me if my work one day met the high standard he has set with his own.

—BRIAN WALKER
BOULDER, COLORADO
1 OCTOBER 1993

Hua Hu Ching

The Unknown Teachings of
LAO TZU

One

I teach the Integral Way of uniting with the great and
  mysterious Tao.
My teachings are simple; if you try to make a religion
  or science of them, they will elude you.
Profound yet plain, they contain the entire truth of
  the universe.

Those who wish to know the whole truth take joy in
  doing the work and service that comes to them.
Having completed it, they take joy in cleansing and
  feeding themselves.
Having cared for others and for themselves, they then
  turn to the master for instruction.

This simple path leads to peace, virtue, and
  abundance.

Two

Men and women who wish to be aware of the whole
    truth should adopt the practices of the Integral
    Way.
These time-honored disciplines calm the mind and
    bring one into harmony with all things.

The first practice is the practice of undiscriminating
    virtue: take care of those who are deserving; also,
    and equally, take care of those who are not.

When you extend your virtue in all directions without
    discriminating, your feet are firmly planted on the
    path that returns to the Tao.

Three

Those who wish to embody the Tao should embrace all things.
To embrace all things means first that one holds no anger or resistance toward any idea or thing, living or dead, formed or formless.
Acceptance is the very essence of the Tao.

To embrace all things means also that one rids oneself of any concept of separation: male and female, self and other, life and death.
Division is contrary to the nature of the Tao.

Foregoing antagonism and separation, one enters into the harmonious oneness of all things.

Four

Every departure from the Tao contaminates one's spirit.

Anger is a departure, resistance a departure, self-absorption a departure.

Over many lifetimes the burden of contaminations can become great.

There is only one way to cleanse oneself of these contaminations, and that is to practice virtue.

What is meant by this?

To practice virtue is to selflessly offer assistance to others, giving without limitation one's time, abilities, and possessions in service, whenever and wherever needed, without prejudice concerning the identity of those in need.

If your willingness to give blessings is limited, so also is your ability to receive them.

This is the subtle operation of the Tao.

Five

Do you imagine the universe is agitated?
Go into the desert at night and look out at the stars.
This practice should answer the question.

The superior person settles her mind as the universe
    settles the stars in the sky.
By connecting her mind with the subtle origin, she
    calms it.
Once calmed, it naturally expands, and ultimately her
    mind becomes as vast and immeasurable as the
    night sky.

Six

The Tao gives rise to all forms, yet it has no form of its
own.
If you attempt to fix a picture of it in your mind, you
will lose it.
This is like pinning a butterfly: the husk is captured,
but the flying is lost.

Why not be content with simply experiencing it?

Seven

The teaching of the Integral Way will go on as long as
   there is a Tao and someone who wishes to embody
   it;
What is painted in these scrolls today will appear in
   different forms in many generations to come.

These things, however, will never change:
Those who wish to attain oneness must practice
   undiscriminating virtue.
They must dissolve all ideas of duality: good and bad,
   beautiful and ugly, high and low.
They will be obliged to abandon any mental bias born
   of cultural or religious belief.
Indeed, they should hold their minds free of any
   thought which interferes with their understanding
   of the universe as a harmonious oneness.

The beginning of these practices is the beginning of
   liberation.

Eight

I confess that there is nothing to teach: no religion, no
science, no body of information which will lead
your mind back to the Tao.
Today I speak in this fashion, tomorrow in another,
but always the Integral Way is beyond words and
beyond mind.

Simply be aware of the oneness of things.

Nine

He who desires the admiration of the world will do
   well to amass a great fortune and then give it away.
The world will respond with admiration in proportion
   to the size of his treasure.
Of course, this is meaningless.

Stop striving after admiration.
Place your esteem on the Tao.
Live in accord with it,
share with others the teachings that lead to it,
and you will be immersed in the blessings that flow
   from it.

Ten

The ego is a monkey catapulting through the jungle:
Totally fascinated by the realm of the senses,
    it swings from one desire to the next,
    one conflict to the next,
    one self-centered idea to the next.
If you threaten it, it actually fears for its life.

Let this monkey go.
Let the senses go.
Let desires go.
Let conflicts go.
Let ideas go.
Let the fiction of life and death go.
Just remain in the center, watching.

And then forget that you are there.

Eleven

Does one scent appeal more than another?
Do you prefer this flavor, or that feeling?
Is your practice sacred and your work profane?
Then your mind is separated:
from itself, from oneness, from the Tao.

Keep your mind free of divisions and distinctions.
When your mind is detached, simple, quiet, then all
things can exist in harmony, and you can begin to
perceive the subtle truth.

Twelve

Do you wish to inhabit sacred space?
To have the respect and companionship of the highest
    spiritual beings?
To be protected by the guardians of the eight powerful
    energy rays?
Then cherish the Integral Way:
Regard these teachings with reverence,
    practice their truths,
      illuminate them to others.

You will receive as many blessings from the universe as
    there are grains of sand in the River of
    Timelessness.

Thirteen

The tiny particles which form the vast universe are not
  tiny at all.
Neither is the vast universe vast.
These are notions of the mind, which is like a knife,
  always chipping away at the Tao,
    trying to render it graspable and manageable.

But that which is beyond form is ungraspable, and
  that which is beyond knowing is unmanageable.
There is, however, this consolation:
She who lets go of the knife will find the Tao at her
  fingertips.

Fourteen

Can you dissolve your ego?
Can you abandon the idea of self and other?
Can you relinquish the notions of male and female,
    short and long, life and death?
Can you let go of all these dualities and embrace the
    Tao without skepticism or panic?
If so, you can reach the heart of the Integral Oneness.

Along the way, avoid thinking of the Oneness as
    unusual, exalted, sublime, transcendental.
Because it is the Oneness, it is beyond all that.
It is simply the direct, essential, and complete truth.

Fifteen

To the ordinary being, others often require tolerance.
To the highly evolved being, there is no such thing as
    tolerance, because there is no such thing as other.
She has given up all ideas of individuality and
    extended her goodwill without prejudice in every
    direction.
Never hating, never resisting, never contesting, she is
    simply always learning and being.

Loving, hating, having expectations:
    all these are attachments.
Attachment prevents the growth of one's true being.
Therefore the integral being is attached to nothing and
    can relate to everyone with an unstructured
    attitude.
Because of this, her very existence benefits all things.

You see, that which has form is equal to that which is
    without form, and that which is alive is equal to
    that which rests.
This is the subtle truth, not a religious invention,
but only those who are already highly evolved will
    understand this.

Sixteen

Most of the world's religions serve only to strengthen
attachments to false concepts such as self and other,
life and death, heaven and earth, and so on.
Those who become entangled in these false ideas are
prevented from perceiving the Integral Oneness.

The highest virtue one can exercise is to accept the
responsibility of discovering and transmitting the
whole truth.
Some help others in order to receive blessings and
admiration.
This is simply meaningless.
Some cultivate themselves in part to serve others, in
part to serve their own pride.
They will understand, at best, half of the truth.
But those who improve themselves for the sake of the
world—to these, the whole truth of the universe
will be revealed.

So seek this whole truth, practice it in your daily life,
and humbly share it with others.
You will enter the realm of the divine.

Seventeen

Do not go about worshipping deities and religious
   institutions as the source of the subtle truth.
To do so is to place intermediaries between yourself
   and the divine, and to make of yourself a beggar
   who looks outside for a treasure that is hidden
   inside his own breast.

If you want to worship the Tao, first discover it in your
   own heart.
Then your worship will be meaningful.

Eighteen

There is no one method for attaining realization of the
    Tao.
To regard any method as *the* method is to create a
    duality, which can only delay your understanding of
    the subtle truth.
The mature person perceives the fruitlessness of rigid,
    external methodologies;
Remembering this, he keeps his attitude unstructured
    at all times and thus is always free to pursue the
    Integral Way.

He studies the teachings of the masters.
He dissolves all concepts of duality.
He pours himself out in service to others.
He performs his inner cleansing and does not disturb
    his teacher with unnecessary entanglements, thus
    preserving the subtle spiritual connection with the
    teacher's divine energy.

Gently eliminating all obstacles to his own
    understanding, he constantly maintains his
    unconditional sincerity.
His humility, perseverance, and adaptability evoke the
    response of the universe and fill him with divine
    light.

Nineteen

To the ordinary person, the body of humanity seems
vast.
In truth, it is neither bigger nor smaller than anything
else.
To the ordinary person, there are others whose
awareness needs raising.
In truth, there is no self, and no other.
To the ordinary person, the temple is sacred and the
field is not.
This, too, is a dualism which runs counter to the
truth.

Those who are highly evolved maintain an
undiscriminating perception.
Seeing everything, labeling nothing, they maintain
their awareness of the Great Oneness.
Thus they are supported by it.

Twenty

The clairvoyant may see forms which are elsewhere,
    but he cannot see the formless.
The telepathic may communicate directly with the
    mind of another, but he cannot communicate with
    one who has achieved no-mind.
The telekinetic may move an object without touching
    it, but he cannot move the intangible.

Such abilities have meaning only in the realm of
    duality.
Therefore, they are meaningless.

Within the Great Oneness, though there is no such
    thing as clairvoyance, telepathy, or telekinesis,
    all things are seen, all things understood,
    all things forever in their proper places.

Twenty-One

Each moment is fragile and fleeting.
The moment of the past cannot be kept, however
    beautiful.
The moment of the present cannot be held, however
    enjoyable.
The moment of the future cannot be caught, however
    desirable.

But the mind is desperate to fix the river in place:
Possessed by ideas of the past, preoccupied with
    images of the future, it overlooks the plain truth of
    the moment.

The one who can dissolve her mind will suddenly
    discover the Tao at her feet, and clarity at hand.

Twenty-Two

How can the divine Oneness be seen?
In beautiful forms, breathtaking wonders, awe-
    inspiring miracles?
The Tao is not obliged to present itself this way.

It is always present and always available.
When speech is exhausted and mind dissolved, it
    presents itself.
When clarity and purity are cultivated, it reveals
    itself.
When sincerity is unconditional, it unveils itself.

If you are willing to be lived by it, you will see it
    everywhere, even in the most ordinary things.

Twenty-Three

The highest truth cannot be put into words.
Therefore the greatest teacher has nothing to say.
He simply gives himself in service, and never worries.

Twenty-Four

Subtle awareness of the truth of the universe should
    not be regarded as an achievement.
To think in terms of achieving it is to place it outside
    your own nature.
This is erroneous and misleading.

Your nature and the integral nature of the universe are
    one and the same: indescribable, but eternally
    present.
Simply open yourself to this.

Twenty-Five

Not all spiritual paths lead to the Harmonious
  Oneness.
Indeed, most are detours and distractions, nothing
  more.
Why not trust the plainness and simplicity of the
  Integral Way?
Living with unconditional sincerity,
  eradicating all duality,
  celebrating the equality of things,
  your every moment will be in truth.

Twenty-Six

There are two kinds of blessings.
The first are worldly blessings, which are won by
doing good deeds.
These concern the mind, and thus are confined in time
and space.
The second is the integral blessing, which falls on
those who achieve awareness of the Great Oneness.
This awareness liberates you from the bondage of
mind, time, and space to fly freely through the
boundless harmony of the Tao.

Similarly, there are two kinds of wisdom.
The first is worldly wisdom, which is a conceptual
understanding of your experiences.
Because it follows after the events themselves, it
necessarily inhibits your direct understanding of
truth.
The second kind, integral wisdom, involves a direct
participation in every moment: the observer and the
observed are dissolved in the light of pure
awareness, and no mental concepts or attitudes are
present to dim that light.

The blessings and wisdom that accrue to those who
practice the Integral Way and lead others to it are a
billion times greater than all worldly blessings and
wisdom combined.

Twenty-Seven

Do not imagine that an integral being has the
    ambition of enlightening the unaware or raising
    worldly people to the divine realm.
To her, there is no self and other, and hence no one to
    be raised; no heaven and hell, and hence no
    destination.
Therefore her only concern is her own sincerity.

Twenty-Eight

It is tempting to view the vast and luminous heavens
   as the body of the Tao.
That would be a mistake, however.
If you identify the Tao with a particular shape, you
   won't ever see it.

Twenty-Nine

Don't think you can attain total awareness and whole
    enlightenment without proper discipline and
    practice.
This is egomania.
Appropriate rituals channel your emotions and life
    energy toward the light.
Without the discipline to practice them, you will
    tumble constantly backward into darkness.

Here is the great secret:
Just as high awareness of the subtle truth is gained
    through virtuous conduct and sustaining
    disciplines, so also is it maintained through these
    things.
Highly evolved beings know and respect the truth of
    this.

Thirty

Words can never convey the beauty of a tree;
   to understand it, you must see it with your own
   eyes.
Language cannot capture the melody of a song;
   to understand it, you must hear it with your own
   ears.
So it is with the Tao: the only way to understand it is
   to directly experience it.

The subtle truth of the universe is unsayable and
   unthinkable.
Therefore the highest teachings are wordless.
My own words are not the medicine, but a
   prescription; not the destination, but a map to help
   you reach it.
When you get there, quiet your mind and close your
   mouth.
Don't analyze the Tao.
Strive instead to live it: silently, undividedly, with
   your whole harmonious being.

Thirty-One

The Tao doesn't come and go.
It is always present everywhere, just like the sky.
If your mind is clouded, you won't see it, but that
    doesn't mean it isn't there.

All misery is created by the activity of the mind.
Can you let go of words and ideas, attitudes and
    expectations?
If so, then the Tao will loom into view.
Can you be still and look inside?
If so, then you will see that the truth is always
    available, always responsive.

Thirty-Two

The ego says that the world is vast, and that the
    particles which form it are tiny.
When tiny particles join, it says, the vast world
    appears.
When the vast world disperses, it says, tiny particles
    appear.

The ego is entranced by all these names and ideas, but
    the subtle truth is that world and particle are the
    same; neither one vast, neither one tiny.
Every thing is equal to every other thing.
Names and concepts only block your perception of this
    Great Oneness.
Therefore it is wise to ignore them.
Those who live inside their egos are continually
    bewildered: they struggle
    frantically to know
    whether things are large or small,
    whether or not there is a purpose
    to joining or dispersing,
    whether the universe is blind and mechanical or the
    divine creation of a conscious being.

In reality there are no grounds for having beliefs or
    making comments about such things.
Look behind them instead, and you will discern the
    deep, silent, complete truth of the Tao.
Embrace it, and your bewilderment vanishes.

Thirty-Three

Just as the world can reveal itself as particles, the Tao
    can reveal itself as human beings.
Though world and particles aren't the same, neither
    are they different.
Though the cosmic body and your body aren't the
    same, neither are they different.

Worlds and particles, bodies and beings, time and
    space:
All are transient expressions of the Tao.
Unseeable, ungraspable, the Tao is beyond any
    attempt to analyze or categorize it.
At the same time, its truth is everywhere you turn.
If you can let go of it with your mind and surround it
    with your heart, it will live inside you forever.

Thirty-Four

All things in the universe move from the subtle to the
    manifest and back again.
Whether the form is that of a star or a person, the
    process is the same.
First, the subtle energy exists.
Next, it becomes manifest and takes on life.
After a time, the life passes away, but the subtle
    energy goes on, either returning to the subtle
    realm, where it remains, or once again attaching to
    manifest things.

The character of your existence is determined by the
    energies to which you connect yourself.
If you attach yourself to gross energies—loving this
    person, hating that clan, rejecting one experience or
    habitually indulging in another—then you will lead
    a series of heavy, attached lives.
This can go on for a very long and tedious time.

The way of the integral being is to join with higher
    things.
By holding to that which is refined and subtle, she
    traverses refined and subtle realms.
If she enters the world, she does so lightly, without
    attachment.
In this way she can go anywhere without ever leaving
    the center of the universe.

Thirty-Five

Intellectual knowledge exists in and of the brain.
Because the brain is part of the body, which must one
day expire, this collection of facts, however large
and impressive, will expire as well.

Insight, however, is a function of the spirit.
Because your spirit follows you through cycle after
cycle of life, death, and rebirth, you have the
opportunity of cultivating insight in an ongoing
fashion.
Refined over time, insight becomes pure, constant,
and unwavering.

This is the beginning of immortality.

Thirty-Six

It is entirely possible for you to achieve immortality,
   and to experience absolute joy and freedom forever.
The practice of undiscriminating virtue is the means
   to this end.

Practicing kindness and selflessness, you naturally
   align your life with the Integral Way.
Aligning your life with the Integral Way, you begin to
   eliminate the illusory boundaries between people
   and societies, between darkness and light, between
   life and death.
Eliminating these illusions, you gain the company of
   the highest spiritual beings.
In their company, you are protected from negative
   influences and your life energy cannot be dissolved.
Thus do you achieve immortality.

Remember: it is not that those who cultivate
   wholeness and virtue in themselves do not encounter
   difficulties in life.
It is that they understand that difficulties are the very
   road to immortality: by meeting them calmly and
   openly, however they unfold, and joyfully
   developing themselves in response to them, they
   become as natural, as complete, and as eternal as the
   Tao itself.

Thirty-Seven

A superior person cares for the well-being of all
   things.
She does this by accepting responsibility for the energy
   she manifests, both actively and in the subtle realm.
Looking at a tree, she sees not an isolated event but
   root, leaves, trunk, water, soil and sun: each event
   related to the others, and "tree" arising out of their
   relatedness.
Looking at herself or another, she sees the same thing.

Trees and animals, humans and insects, flowers and
   birds:
These are active images of the subtle energies that flow
   from the stars throughout the universe. Meeting
   and combining with each other and the elements of
   the earth, they give rise to all living things.

The superior person understands this, and understands
   that her own energies play a part in it.
Understanding these things, she respects the earth as
   her mother, the heavens as her father, and all living
   things as her brothers and sisters.

Caring for them, she knows that she cares for herself.
Giving to them, she knows that she gives to herself.
At peace with them, she is always at peace with
   herself.

Thirty-Eight

Why scurry about looking for the truth?
It vibrates in every thing and every not-thing, right off
the tip of your nose.
Can you be still and see it in the mountain? the pine
tree? yourself?

Don't imagine that you'll discover it by accumulating
more knowledge.
Knowledge creates doubt, and doubt makes you
ravenous for more knowledge.
You can't get full eating this way.
The wise person dines on something more subtle:
He eats the understanding that the named was born
from the unnamed, that all being flows from non-
being, that the describable world emanates from an
indescribable source.
He finds this subtle truth inside his own self, and
becomes completely content.

So who can be still and watch the chess game of the
world?
The foolish are always making impulsive moves, but
the wise know that victory and defeat are decided by
something more subtle.
They see that something perfect exists before any move
is made.

This subtle perfection deteriorates when artificial
   actions are taken, so be content not to disturb the
   peace.
Remain quiet.
Discover the harmony in your own being.
Embrace it.

If you can do this, you will gain everything, and the
   world will become healthy again.
If you can't, you will be lost in the shadows forever.

Thirty-Nine

If you go searching for the Great Creator, you will
   come back empty-handed.
The source of the universe is ultimately unknowable, a
   great invisible river flowing forever through a vast
   and fertile valley.
Silent and uncreated, it creates all things.

All things are brought forth from the subtle realm into
   the manifest world by the mystical intercourse of
   yin and yang.
The dynamic river yang pushes forward, the still valley
   yin is receptive, and through their integration
   things come into existence.
This is known as the Great Tai Chi.

Tai chi is the integral truth of the universe.
Everything is a tai chi: your body, the cosmic body,
   form, appearance, wisdom, energy, the unions of
   people, the dispersal of time and places.
Each brings itself into existence through the
   integration of yin and yang, maintains itself, and
   disperses itself without the direction of any creator.
Your creation, your self-transformation, the
   accumulation of energy and wisdom, the decline
   and cessation of your body: all these take place by
   themselves within the subtle operation of the
   universe.

Therefore agitated effort is not necessary.
Just be aware of the Great Tai Chi.

Forty

The natural laws of the universe are inviolable:
Energy condenses into substance.
Food is eaten through the mouth and not the nose.
A person who neglects to breathe will turn blue and
 die.
Some things simply can't be dismissed.

It is also a part of the cosmic law that what you say
 and do determines what happens in your life.
The ordinary person thinks that this law is external to
 himself and he feels confined and controlled by it.
So his desires trouble his mind, his mind troubles his
 spirit, and he lives in constant turmoil with himself
 and the world.
His whole life is spent in struggling.

The superior person recognizes that he and the subtle
 law are one.
Therefore he cultivates himself to accord with it,
 bringing moderation to his actions and clarity to his
 mind.
Doing this, he finds himself at one with all that is
 divine and enlightened.
His days are passed drinking in serenity and breathing
 out contentment.

This is the profound, simple truth:
You are the master of your life and death.
What you do is what you are.

Forty-One

Good and bad, self and others, life and death:
Why affirm these concepts? Why deny them?
To do either is to exercise the mind, and the integral
    being knows that the manipulations of the mind are
    dreams, delusions, and shadows.

Hold one idea, and another competes with it.
Soon the two will be in conflict with a third, and in
    time your life is all chatter and contradiction.

Seek instead to keep your mind undivided.
Dissolve all ideas into the Tao.

Forty-Two

Nothing in the realm of thoughts or ideologies is
  absolute.
Lean on one for long, and it collapses.
Because of this, there is nothing more futile and
  frustrating than relying on the mind.

To arrive at the unshakable, you must befriend the
  Tao.
To do this, quiet your thinking.
Stop analyzing, dividing, making distinctions between
  one thing and another.
Simply see that you are at the center of the universe,
  and accept all things and beings as parts of your
  infinite body.

When you perceive that an act done to another is done
  to yourself, you have understood the great truth.

Forty-Three

In ancient times, people lived holistic lives.

They didn't overemphasize the intellect, but
integrated mind, body, and spirit in all things.

This allowed them to become masters of knowledge
rather than victims of concepts.

If a new invention appeared, they looked for the
troubles it might cause as well as the shortcuts it
offered.

They valued old ways that had been proven effective,
and they valued new ways if they could be proven
effective.

If you want to stop being confused, then emulate these
ancient folk: join your body, mind, and spirit in all
you do.

Choose food, clothing, and shelter that accords with
nature.

Rely on your own body for transportation.

Allow your work and your recreation to be one and the
same.

Do exercise that develops your whole being and not
just your body.

Listen to music that bridges the three spheres of your
being.

Choose leaders for their virtue rather than their wealth
or power.

Serve others and cultivate yourself simultaneously.

Understand that true growth comes from meeting and
solving the problems of life in a way that is
harmonizing to yourself and to others.

If you can follow these simple old ways, you will be
continually renewed.

Forty-Four

This is the nature of the unenlightened mind:
The sense organs, which are limited in scope and
　　ability, randomly gather information.
This partial information is arranged into judgements,
　　which are based on previous judgements,
　　which are usually based on someone else's foolish
　　ideas.
These false concepts and ideas are then stored in a
　　highly selective memory system.

Distortion upon distortion: the mental energy flows
　　constantly through contorted and inappropriate
　　channels, and the more one uses the mind, the more
　　confused one becomes.

To eliminate the vexation of the mind, it doesn't help
　　to *do* something; this only reinforces the mind's
　　mechanics.
Dissolving the mind is instead a matter of not-doing:
Simply avoid becoming attached to what you see and
　　think.
Relinquish the notion that you are separated from the
　　all-knowing mind of the universe.
Then you can recover your original pure insight and
　　see through all illusions.
Knowing nothing, you will be aware of everything.

Remember: because clarity and enlightenment are
　　within your own nature, they are regained without
　　moving an inch.

Forty-Five

If you correct your mind, the rest of your life will fall
    into place.
This is true because the mind is the governing aspect
    of a human life.
If the river flows clearly and cleanly through the
    proper channel, all will be well along its banks.

The Integral Way depends on decreasing, not
    increasing:
To correct your mind, rely on not-doing.
Stop thinking and clinging to complications;
    keep your mind detached and whole.
Eliminate mental muddiness and obscurity;
    keep your mind crystal clear.
Avoid daydreaming and allow your pure original
    insight to emerge.
Quiet your emotions and abide in serenity.
Don't go crazy with the worship of idols, images, and
    ideas; this is like putting a new head on top of the
    head you already have.

Remember: if you can cease all restless activity, your
    integral nature will appear.

Forty-Six

The Tao gives birth to One.
One gives birth to yin and yang.
Yin and yang give birth to all things.
Now forget this.

The complete whole is the complete whole.
So also is any part the complete whole.
Forget this, too.

Pain and happiness are simply conditions of the ego.
Forget the ego.

Time and space are changing and dissolving, not fixed
    and real.
They can be thought of as accessories, but don't think
    of them.

Supernatural beings without form extend their life
    force throughout the universe to support beings
    both formed and unformed.
But never mind this; the supernatural is just a part of
    nature, like the natural.
The subtle truth emphasizes neither and includes
    both.

All truth is in tai chi: to cultivate the mind, body, or
    spirit, simply balance the polarities.
If people understood this, world peace and universal
    harmony would naturally arise.

But forget about understanding and harmonizing and
   making all things one.
The universe is already a harmonious oneness; just
   realize it.

If you scramble about in search of inner peace, you
   will lose your inner peace.

Forty-Seven

Dualistic thinking is a sickness.
Religion is a distortion.
Materialism is cruel.
Blind spirituality is unreal.

Chanting is no more holy than listening to the
    murmur of a stream, counting prayer beads no more
    sacred than simply breathing, religious robes no
    more spiritual than work clothes.

If you wish to attain oneness with the Tao, don't get
    caught up in spiritual superficialities.
Instead, live a quiet and simple life, free of ideas and
    concepts.
Find contentment in the practice of undiscriminating
    virtue, the only true power.
Giving to others selflessly and anonymously, radiating
    light throughout the world and illuminating your
    own darknesses, your virtue becomes a sanctuary for
    yourself and all beings.

This is what is meant by embodying the Tao.

Forty-Eight

Do you wish to free yourself of mental and emotional
    knots and become one with the Tao?
If so, there are two paths available to you.

The first is the path of acceptance.
Affirm everyone and everything.
Freely extend your goodwill and virtue in every
    direction, regardless of circumstances.
Embrace all things as part of the Harmonious
    Oneness, and then you will begin to perceive it.

The second path is that of denial.
Recognize that everything you see and think is a
    falsehood, an illusion, a veil over the truth.
Peel all the veils away, and you will arrive at the
    Oneness.

Though these paths are entirely different, they will
    deliver you to the same place: spontaneous
    awareness of the Great Oneness.
Once you arrive there, remember: it isn't necessary to
    struggle to maintain unity with it.

All you have to do is participate in it.

Forty-Nine

Thinking and talking about the Integral Way are not
the same as practicing it.
Who ever became a good rider by talking about
horses?
If you wish to embody the Tao, stop chattering and
start practicing.
Relax your body and quiet your senses.
Return your mind to its original clarity.
Forget about being separated from others and from the
Divine Source.

As you return to the Oneness, do not think of it or be
in awe of it. This is just another way of separating
from it.
Simply merge into truth, and allow it to surround
you.

Fifty

What good is it to spend your life accumulating
    material things?
It isn't in keeping with the Tao.
What benefit in conforming your behavior to
    someone's conventions?
It violates your nature and dissipates your energy.
Why separate your spiritual life and your practical life?
To an integral being, there is no such distinction.

Live simply and virtuously, true to your nature,
    drawing no line between what is spiritual and what
    is not.

Ignore time.
Relinquish ideas and concepts.
Embrace the Oneness.

This is the Integral Way.

Fifty-One

Those who want to know the truth of the universe
  should practice the four cardinal virtues.

The first is reverence for all life; this manifests as
  unconditional love and respect for oneself and all
  other beings.
The second is natural sincerity; this manifests as
  honesty, simplicity, and faithfulness.
The third is gentleness; this manifests as kindness,
  consideration for others, and sensitivity to spiritual
  truth.
The fourth is supportiveness; this manifests as service
  to others without expectation of reward.

The four virtues are not an external dogma but a part
  of your original nature.
When practiced, they give birth to wisdom and evoke
  the five blessings: health, wealth, happiness,
  longevity, and peace.

Fifty-Two

Do you think you can clear your mind by sitting
    constantly in silent meditation?
This makes your mind narrow, not clear.
Integral awareness is fluid and adaptable, present
    in all places and at all times.
That is true meditation.

Who can attain clarity and simplicity by avoiding the
    world?
The Tao is clear and simple, and it doesn't avoid the
    world.

Why not simply honor your parents,
    love your children,
    help your brothers and sisters,
    be faithful to your friends,
    care for your mate with devotion,
    complete your work cooperatively and joyfully,
    assume responsibility for problems,
    practice virtue without first demanding it of others,
    understand the highest truths yet retain an ordinary
        manner?

That would be true clarity, true simplicity, true
    mastery.

Fifty-Three

True understanding in a person has two attributes:
  awareness and action.
Together they form a natural tai chi.

Who can enjoy enlightenment and remain indifferent
  to suffering in the world?
This is not in keeping with the Way.
Only those who increase their service along with their
  understanding can be called men and women of
  Tao.

Fifty-Four

In ancient times, various holistic sciences were
   developed by highly evolved beings to enable their
   own evolution and that of others.
These subtle arts were created through the linking of
   individual minds with the universal mind.
They are still taught by traditional teachers to those
   who display virtue and desire to assist others.

The student who seeks out and studies these teachings
   furthers the evolution of mankind as well as her own
   spiritual unfolding.
The student who ignores them hinders the
   development of all beings.

Fifty-Five

The holistic practices of the ancient masters integrate
science, art, and personal spiritual development.
Mind, body, and spirit participate in them equally.
They include:

1. Yi Yau, the healing science which incorporates
   diagnosis, acupuncture, herbal medicine,
   therapeutic diet, and other methods;
2. Syang Ming, the science which predicts a
   person's destiny by observing the outward
   physical manifestations of his face, skeleton,
   palms, and voice;
3. Feng Shui, the science of discerning the subtle
   energy rays present in a geographic location to
   determine whether they will properly support
   the activities of a building or town constructed
   there;
4. Fu Kua, the observation of the subtle alterations
   of yin and yang for the purpose of making
   decisions which are harmonious with the
   apparent and hidden aspects of a situation. The
   foundation of Fu Kua and of all Taoist practice
   is the study of the I Ching, or Book of Changes.
5. Nei Dan, Wai Dan, and Fang Jung, the
   sciences of refining one's personal energy
   through alchemy, chemistry, and the cultivation
   of balanced sexual energy;
6. Tai Syi, the science of revitalization through
   breathing and visualization techniques;

7. Chwun Shi, the transformation of one's spiritual essence through keeping one's thoughts in accord with the Divine Source;

8. Shu-Ser, the attunement of one's daily life to the cycle of universal energy rays;

9. Bi Gu, the practice of fasting on specific days in order to gather life energy emanating from the harmonized positions of certain stars;

10. Sau Yi, the science of embracing integral transcendental oneness in order to accomplish conception of the 'mystical pearl';

11. Tai Chi Ch'uan, the performance of physical exercises to induce and direct energy flows within the body to gain mastery of body, breath, mind, the internal organs, and life and death;

12. Fu Chi, the science of reforming and refining one's energy with pure food and herbs;

13. Chuan Se, the inner visualization of the unity of one's inner and outer being;

14. 'Dzai Jing, the purification of one's energy through ascetic practices;

15. Fu Jou, the drawing of mystical pictures and the writing and recital of mystical invocations for the purpose of evoking a response from the subtle realm of the universe;

16. Tsan Syan, the process of dissolving the ego and connecting with the Great Oneness through the study of classical scriptures and daily dialogue with an enlightened master;

17. Lyou Yen and Chi Men, the mystical sciences of energy linkage for the purpose of influencing external affairs.

Of these, the most important for beginners is the study of the I Ching, which enables one to perceive the hidden influences in every situation and thus establish a balanced and spiritually evolved means of responding to them.

All are instruments for attaining the Tao.
To study them is to serve universal unity, harmony, and wisdom.

Fifty-Six

If you wish to become a person of Tao, then study that
which serves the nature of life, and offer it to the
world.
Allow your devotion to learning the Taoist ways to be
complete.
Partial practice and partial discipline won't do:
You can't know the body by studying the finger, and
you can't understand the universe by learning one
science.
If you study the whole of the Tao wholeheartedly,
then everything in your life will reflect it.

Fifty-Seven

The universe is a vast net of energy rays.

The primary ray is that which emanates from the
  Subtle Origin, and it is entirely positive, creative,
  and constructive.

Each being, however, converts the energy of this
  primary ray into its own ray, and these lower rays
  can be either positive or negative, constructive or
  destructive.

An individual who is not yet fully evolved can be
  adversely affected by negative energy rays in the net
  around him.

For example, the combined influence of several
  negative rays might cause an undeveloped person to
  believe that his life is being controlled by an
  invisible, oppressive ruler.

Such a misconception can be a significant barrier to
  enlightenment.

To attain full evolution and the status of an integral
  being, you must be aware of this intricate net and
  its influences upon you.

By integrating the positive, harmonious energy rays
  with the positive elements of your own being, and
  eliminating the subtle negative influences, you can
  enhance all aspects of your life.

In order to eliminate the negative influences, simply
  ignore them.

To integrate the positive influences, consciously
   reconnect yourself with the primary energy ray of
   the Subtle Origin by adopting the practices of the
   Integral Way.
Then all the rays in the net around you will merge
   back into harmonious oneness.

Fifty-Eight

Unless the mind, body, and spirit are equally
   developed and fully integrated, no spiritual peak or
   state of enlightenment can be sustained.
This is why extremist religions and ideologies do not
   bear fruit.

When the mind and spirit are forced into unnatural
   austerities or adherence to external dogmas, the
   body grows sick and weak and becomes a traitor to
   the whole being.
When the body is emphasized to the exclusion of the
   mind and spirit, they become like trapped snakes:
   frantic, explosive, and poisonous to one's person.
All such imbalances inevitably lead to exhaustion and
   expiration of the life force.

True self-cultivation involves the holistic integration of
   mind, body, and spirit.
Balancing yin and yang through the various practices
   of the Integral Way, one achieves complete unity
   within and without.
This manifests in the world as perfect equilibrium,
   and perfect grace.

Fifty-Nine

Greed for enlightenment and immortality is no
different than greed for material wealth.
It is self-centered and dualistic, and thus an obstacle to
true attainment.
Therefore these states are never achieved by those who
covet them; rather, they are the reward of the
virtuous.

If you wish to become a divine immortal angel, then
restore the angelic qualities of your being through
virtue and service.
This is the only way to gain the attention of the
immortals who teach the methods of energy
enhancement and integration that are necessary to
reach the divine realm.

These angelic teachers cannot be sought out; it is they
who seek out the student.
When you succeed in connecting your energy with the
divine realm through high awareness and the
practice of undiscriminating virtue, the
transmission of the ultimate subtle truths will
follow.
This is the path that all angels take to the divine
realm.

Sixty

The mystical techniques for achieving immortality are
revealed only to those who have dissolved all ties to
the gross worldly realm of duality, conflict, and
dogma.
As long as your shallow worldly ambitions exist, the
door will not open.

Devote yourself to living a virtuous, integrated,
selfless life.
Refine your energy from gross and heavy to subtle and
light.
Use the practices of the Integral Way to transform
your superficial worldly personality into a profound,
divine presence.

By going through each stage of development along the
Integral Way, you learn to value what is important
today in the subtle realm rather than what appears
desirable tomorrow in the worldly realm.

Then the mystical door will open, and you can join the
unruling rulers and uncreating creators of the vast
universe.

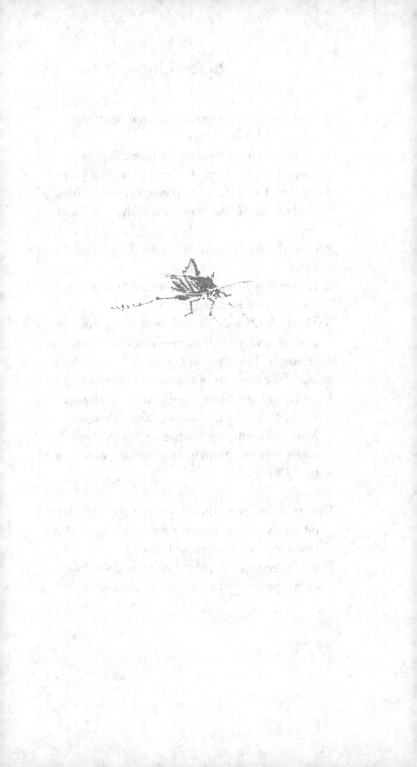

Sixty-One

To understand the universe, you must study and
   understand these things:
First, the Oneness, the Tao, the Great Tai Chi;
Second, the Great Two, the forces of yin and yang;
Third, the Three Main Categories, expressed either as
   Heaven, Earth, and Man, or as body, mind, and
   spirit;
Fourth, the Four Forces, strong, weak, light, and
   heavy;
Fifth, the Five Elements, symbolized by water, fire,
   wood, metal, and earth;
Sixth, the Six Breaths—wind, cold, heat, moisture,
   dryness, and inflammation—which transform the
   climate and the internal organs;
Seventh, the processes of change and recycling;
Eighth, the Eight Great Manifestations—Heaven,
   Earth, Water, Fire, Thunder, Lake, Wind, and
   Mountain—the combinations of which reveal the
   subtle energetic truth of all situations, as taught in
   the I Ching.

Understanding these things, you can employ them
   internally to leave behind what is old and dead and
   to embrace what is new and alive.
Once discovered, this process of internal alchemy
   opens the mystical gate to spiritual immortality.

Sixty-Two

Do you wish to attain pure Tao?
Then you must understand and integrate within
   yourself the three main energies of the universe.

The first is the earth energy.
Centered in the belly, it expresses itself as sexuality.
Those who cultivate and master the physical energy
   attain partial purity.

The second is the heaven energy.
Centered in the mind, it expresses itself as knowledge
   and wisdom.
Those whose minds merge with the Universal Mind
   also attain partial purity.

The third is the harmonized energy.
Centered in the heart, it expresses itself as spiritual
   insight.
Those who develop spiritual insight also attain partial
   purity.

Only when you achieve all three—mastery of the
   physical energy, universal mindedness, and spiritual
   insight—and express them in a virtuous integral
   life, can you attain pure Tao.

Sixty-Three

There are three layers to the universe:
In the lower, Tai Ching, and the middle, Shan Ching,
the hindrance of a physical bodily existence is
required.
Those who fail to live consistently in accord with Tao
reside here.

In the upper, Yu Ching, there is only Tao: the bondage
of form is broken, and the only thing existing is the
exquisite energy dance of the immortal divine
beings.

Those who wish to enter Yu Ching should follow the
Integral Way.
Simplify the personality, refine the sexual energy
upward, integrate yin and yang in body, mind, and
spirit, practice non-impulsiveness, make your
conscience one with pure law, and you will uncover
truth after truth and enter the exquisite upper
realm.

This path is clearly defined and quite simple to follow,
yet most lose themselves in ideological fogs of their
own making.

Sixty-Four

In earlier times, people lived simply and serenely.
Sensitive to the fluctuations that constantly occur, they
were able to adjust comfortably to the energy of the
day.

Today, people lead hysterical, impulsive lives.
Ignoring the subtle alterations of yin and yang which
influence all things, they become confused,
exhausted, and frustrated.
However, even today one can restore wholeness and
clarity to one's mind.
The way to do this is through study of the I Ching.

Like the cycle of day and night, everything is a tai chi
incorporating movements between yin and yang.
If you do not see the patterns in these movements, you
are lost.
But if you consult the I Ching with an open mind,
you will begin to see the patterns underlying all
things.
Knowing that daybreak will come, you can rest
peacefully at night.

When you accurately perceive the fluidity of things,
you also begin to perceive the constancy behind
them: the creative, transformative, boundless,
immutable Tao.
To see this is the ultimate education, and the ultimate
solace.

Sixty-Five

The interplay of yin and yang within the womb of the
   Mysterious Mother creates the expansion and
   contraction of nature.
Although the entire universe is created out of this
   reproductive dance, it is but a tiny portion of her
   being.
Her heart is the Universal Heart, and her mind the
   Universal Mind.

The reproductive function is also a part of human
   beings.
Because yin and yang are not complete within us as
   individuals, we pair up to integrate them and bring
   forth new life.
Although most people spend their entire lives
   following this biological impulse, it is only a tiny
   portion of our beings as well.
If we remain obsessed with seeds and eggs, we are
   married to the fertile reproductive valley of the
   Mysterious Mother but not to her immeasurable
   heart and all-knowing mind.

If you wish to unite with her heart and mind, you
   must integrate yin and yang within and refine their
   fire upward.
Then you have the power to merge with the whole
   being of the Mysterious Mother.

This is what is known as true evolution.

Sixty-Six

The first integration of yin and yang is the union of
    seed and egg within the womb.
The second integration of yin and yang is the sexual
    union of the mature male and female.
Both of these are concerned with flesh and blood, and
    all that is conceived in this realm must one day
    disintegrate and pass away.

It is only the third integration which gives birth to
    something immortal.
In this integration, a highly evolved individual joins
    the subtle inner energies of yin and yang under the
    light of spiritual understanding.
Through the practices of the Integral Way he refines
    his gross, heavy energy into something ethereal and
    light.
This divine light has the capability of penetrating into
    the mighty ocean of spiritual energy and complete
    wisdom that is the Tao.

The new life created by the final integration is self-
    aware yet without ego, capable of inhabiting a body
    yet not attached to it, and guided by wisdom rather
    than emotion.
Whole and virtuous, it can never die.

Sixty-Seven

To achieve the highest levels of life, one must
    continually combine new levels of yin and yang.
In nature, the male energy can be found in such
    sources as the sun and the mountains, and the
    female in such sources as the earth, the moon, and
    the lakes.
Those who study these things, which are only hinted
    at here, will benefit immeasurably.

Because higher and higher unions of yin and yang are
    necessary for the conception of higher life, some
    students may be instructed in the art of dual
    cultivation, in which yin and yang are directly
    integrated in the tai chi of sexual intercourse.
If the student is not genuinely virtuous and the
    instruction not that of a true master, dual
    cultivation can have a destructive effect.
If genuine virtue and true mastery come together,
    however, the practice can bring about a profound
    balancing of the student's gross and subtle energies.
The result of this is improved health, harmonized
    emotions, the cessation of desires and impulses,
    and, at the highest level, the transcendent
    integration of the entire energy body.

Sixty-Eight

In angelic dual cultivation, one learns to follow the
Tao.
To approach the Tao, you will need all your sincerity,
for it is elusive, first revealing itself in form and
image, then dissolving into subtle, indefinable
essence.

Though it is uncreated itself, it creates all things.
Because it has no substance, it can enter into where
there is no space.
Exercising by returning to itself, winning victories by
remaining gentle and yielding, it is softer than
anything, and therefore it overcomes everything
hard.

What does this tell you about the benefit of non-action
and silence?

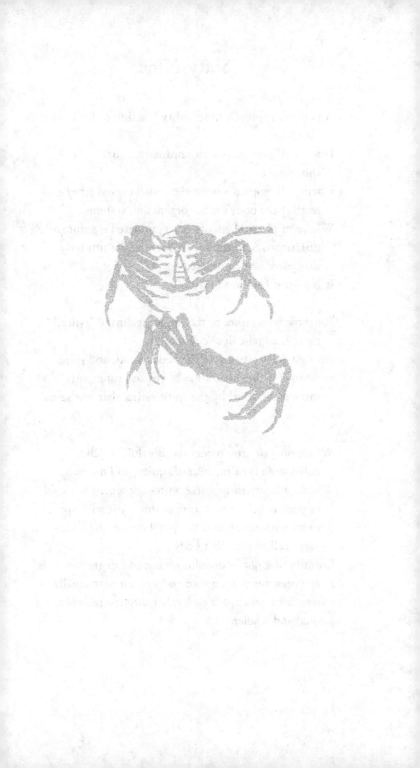

Sixty-Nine

A person's approach to sexuality is a sign of his level of
 evolution.
Unevolved persons practice ordinary sexual
 intercourse.
Placing all emphasis upon the sexual organs, they
 neglect the body's other organs and systems.
Whatever physical energy is accumulated is summarily
 discharged, and the subtle energies are similarly
 dissipated and disordered.
It is a great backward leap.

For those who aspire to the higher realms of living,
 there is angelic dual cultivation.
Because every portion of the body, mind, and spirit
 yearns for the integration of yin and yang, angelic
 intercourse is led by the spirit rather than the sexual
 organs.

Where ordinary intercourse is effortful, angelic
 cultivation is calm, relaxed, quiet, and natural.
Where ordinary intercourse unites sex organs with sex
 organs, angelic cultivation unites spirit with spirit,
 mind with mind, and every cell of one body with
 every cell of the other body.
Culminating not in dissolution but in integration, it is
 an opportunity for a man and woman to mutually
 transform and uplift each other into the realm of
 bliss and wholeness.

The sacred ways of angelic intercourse are taught only
by one who has himself achieved total energy
integration, and taught only to students who follow
the Integral Way with profound devotion, seeking
to purify and pacify the entire world along with
their own being.

However, if your virtue is especially radiant, it can be
possible to open a pathway to the subtle realm and
receive these celestial teachings directly from the
immortals.

Seventy

The cords of passion and desire weave a binding net
    around you.
Worldly confrontation makes you stiff and inflexible.
The trap of duality is tenacious.
Bound, rigid, and trapped, you cannot experience
    liberation.

Through dual cultivation it is possible to unravel the
    net, soften the rigidity, dismantle the trap.
Dissolving your yin energy into the source of universal
    life, attracting the yang energy from that same
    source, you leave behind individuality and your life
    becomes pure nature.
Free of ego, living naturally, working virtuously, you
    become filled with inexhaustible vitality and are
    liberated forever from the cycle of death and
    rebirth.

Understand this if nothing else: spiritual freedom
    and oneness with the Tao are not randomly
    bestowed gifts, but the rewards of conscious
    self-transformation and self-evolution.

Seventy-One

The transformation toward eternal life is gradual.
The heavy, gross energy of body, mind, and spirit
    must first be purified and uplifted.
When the energy ascends to the subtle level, then
    self-mastery can be sought.

A wise instructor teaches the powerful principles of
    self-integration only to those who have already
    achieved a high level of self-purification and
    self-mastery.
In addition, all proper teaching follows the law of
    energy response: the most effective method is always
    that to which the student's natural energy most
    harmoniously responds.
For one, celibacy and self-cultivation will be
    appropriate; for another, properly guided dual
    cultivation will derive the greatest benefit.
A discerning teacher will determine the proper balance
    of practices for each individual.

In any case, know that all teachers and techniques are
    only transitional: true realization comes from the
    direct merger of one's being with the divine energy
    of the Tao.

Seventy-Two

If you wish to gain merit and become one with the
divine, then develop your virtue and extend it to the
world.
Abandon fancy theologies and imaginary ideas and do
some ordinary daily work, such as healing.
Let go of all conflict and strife.
Practice unswerving kindness and unending patience.
Avoid following impulses and pursuing ambitions
which destroy the wholeness of your mind and
separate you from the Integral Way.
Neither become obsessed with circumstances nor
forego awareness of them.
To manage your mind, know that there is nothing,
and then relinquish all attachment to the
nothingness.

Seventy-Three

The teacher cannot aid the student as long as the
  student's spirit is contaminated.
The cleansing of the spiritual contamination is not the
  responsibility of the teacher, but of the student.
It is accomplished by offering one's talent, resources,
  and life to the world.
Also, to the teacher and to the immortal angels that
  surround him, a healthy student can offer his pure
  energy, and a depleted student can give at the very
  least food, or wine, or service.

When one gives whatever one can without restraint,
  the barriers of individuality break down.
It no longer becomes possible to tell whether it is the
  student offering himself to the teacher, or the
  teacher offering herself to the student.
One sees only two immaculate beings, reflecting one
  another like a pair of brilliant mirrors.

Seventy-Four

There are those who derive energy from worshipping
 and meditating on divine beings and deities.
If you feel inclined to worship, then worship these:

Worship the fiery sun, repository of yang, and the
 watery moon, repository of yin;

Worship the spiritual centers of men and women,
 which are angelic in every sense;

Worship the Eight Great Manifestations: Heaven,
 Earth, Water, Fire, Thunder, Lake, Wind, and
 Mountain;

Worship the sixty-four hexagrams of the I Ching,
 which illuminate the underlying harmony of the
 universe;

Finally, worship the Great Tai Chi, in which all things
 are contained, balanced, and reposed.

Seventy-Five

Would you like to liberate yourself from the lower
realms of life?
Would you like to save the world from the degradation
and destruction it seems destined for?
Then step away from shallow mass movements and
quietly go to work on your own self-awareness.

If you want to awaken all of humanity, then awaken
all of yourself.
If you want to eliminate the suffering in the world,
then eliminate all that is dark and negative in
yourself.
Truly, the greatest gift you have to give is that of your
own self-transformation.

So find a teacher who is an integral being, a beacon
who extends his light and virtue with equal ease to
those who appreciate him and those who don't.
Shape yourself in his mold, bathe in his nourishing
radiance, and reflect it out to the rest of the world.
You will come to understand an eternal truth: there is
always a peaceful home for a virtuous being.

Seventy-Six

Who can save the world?

Perhaps one who devotedly follows these teachings,
　　who calms her mind,
　　　　who ignores all divergence, who develops a high
　　　　　　awareness of the subtle truths,
　　　　who merges her virtue with the universal virtue and
　　　　　　extends it to the world without expectation of
　　　　　　reward.

She will indeed be the savior of the world.

Seventy-Seven

Humanity grows more and more intelligent, yet there
 is clearly more trouble and less happiness daily.
How can this be so?
It is because intelligence is not the same thing as
 wisdom.

When a society misuses partial intelligence and
 ignores holistic wisdom, its people forget the
 benefits of a plain and natural life.
Seduced by their desires, emotions, and egos, they
 become slaves to bodily demands, to luxuries, to
 power and unbalanced religion and psychological
 excuses.
Then the reign of calamity and confusion begins.

Nonetheless, superior people can awaken during times
 of turmoil to lead others out of the mire.
But how can the one liberate the many?
By first liberating his own being.
He does this not by elevating himself, but by lowering
 himself.
He lowers himself to that which is simple, modest,
 true; integrating it into himself, he becomes a
 master of simplicity, modesty, truth.

Completely emancipated from his former false life, he
 discovers his original pure nature, which is the pure
 nature of the universe.

Freely and spontaneously releasing his divine energy,
   he constantly transcends complicated situations and
   draws everything around him back into an integral
   oneness.
Because he is a living divinity, when he acts, the
   universe acts.

Seventy-Eight

There are many partial religions, and then there is the
   Integral Way.
Partial religions are desperate, clever, human
   inventions; the Integral Way is a deep expression of
   the pure, whole, universal mind.
Partial religions rely on the hypnotic manipulation of
   undeveloped minds; the Integral Way is founded on
   the free transmission of the plain, natural,
   immutable truth.
It is a total reality, not an occult practice.

The Integral Way eschews conceptual fanaticism,
   extravagant living, fancy food, violent music.
They spoil the serenity of one's mind and obstruct
   one's spiritual development.
Renouncing what is fashionable and embracing what is
   plain, honest, and virtuous, the Integral Way
   returns you to the subtle essence of life.
Adopt its practices and you will become like they are:
   honest, simple, true, virtuous, whole.

You see, in partial pursuits, one's transformation is
   always partial as well.
But in integral self-cultivation, it is possible to achieve
   a complete metamorphosis, to transcend your
   emotional and biological limitations and evolve to a
   higher state of being.

By staying out of the shadows and following this
    simple path, you become extraordinary,
    unfathomable, a being of profound cosmic subtlety.
You outlive time and space by realizing the subtle
    truth of the universe.

Seventy-Nine

Those in future generations who study and practice the
truth of these teachings will be blessed.
They will acquire the subtle light of wisdom, the
mighty sword of clarity that cuts through all
obstruction, and the mystical pearl of
understanding that envelops the entire universe.
They will attain the insight necessary to perceive the
integral truth of the Tao.
Following this truth with unabashed sincerity, they
will become it: whole, courageous, indestructible,
unnameable.

Eighty

The world is full of half-enlightened masters.
Overly clever, too "sensitive" to live in the real world,
    they surround themselves with selfish pleasures and
    bestow their grandiose teachings upon the unwary.
Prematurely publicizing themselves, intent upon
    reaching some spiritual climax, they constantly
    sacrifice the truth and deviate from the Tao.
What they really offer the world is their own
    confusion.

The true master understands that enlightenment is not
    the end, but the means.
Realizing that virtue is her goal, she accepts the long
    and often arduous cultivation that is necessary to
    attain it.
She doesn't scheme to become a leader, but quietly
    shoulders whatever responsibilities fall to her.

Unattached to her accomplishments, taking credit for
    nothing at all, she guides the whole world by
    guiding the individuals who come to her.
She shares her divine energy with her students,
    encouraging them, creating trials to strengthen
    them, scolding them to awaken them, directing the
    streams of their lives toward the infinite ocean of
    the Tao.

If you aspire to this sort of mastery, then root yourself
    in the Tao.

Relinquish your negative habits and attitudes.

Strengthen your sincerity.

Live in the real world, and extend your virtue to it without discrimination in the daily round.

Be the truest father or mother, the truest brother or sister, the truest friend, and the truest disciple.

Humbly respect and serve your teacher, and dedicate your entire being unwaveringly to self-cultivation.

Then you will surely achieve self-mastery and be able to help others in doing the same.

Eighty-One

With all this talking, what has been said?
The subtle truth can be pointed at with words, but it
can't be contained by them.

Take time to listen to what is said without words, to
obey the law too subtle to be written, to worship
the unnameable and to embrace the unformed.
Love your life.
Trust the Tao.
Make love with the invisible subtle origin of the
universe, and you will give yourself everything you
need.

You won't have to hide away forever in spiritual
retreats.
You can be a gentle, contemplative hermit right here
in the middle of everything, utterly unaffected,
thoroughly sustained and rewarded by your integral
practices.

Encouraging others, giving freely to all, awakening
and purifying the world with each movement and
action, you'll ascend to the divine realm in broad
daylight.

The breath of the Tao speaks, and those who are in
harmony with it hear quite clearly.

BRIAN WALKER IS THE AUTHOR OF *THE I CHING*
AND *THE CRAZY DOG GUIDE TO LIFETIME HAPPINESS*.
HE LIVES IN BOULDER, COLORADO.

JACKET PAINTING: *RAINSTORM OVER PARADISE VALLEY*,
BY RUSSELL CHATHAM.
JACKET DESIGN BY ANNE GARNER.
BOOK DESIGN BY STACY FELDMANN AND JAMIE POTENBERG.
COMPOSED IN GARAMOND #3
BY WILSTED & TAYLOR, OAKLAND.